D1133217

CHARLOTTE: A DIARY IN PICTURES

CHARLOTTE
A DIARY IN PICTURES

by
CHARLOTTE SALOMON

Comment by Paul Tillich

Biographical Note by Emil Straus

A HELEN AND KURT WOLFF BOOK

HARCOURT, BRACE & WORLD, INC., NEW YORK

Grateful acknowledgment is made to Mr. and Mrs. Albert Salomon
and to the Stedelijk Museum, Amsterdam,
for permission to publish Charlotte Salomon's paintings, and to
A. J. Petersen, Curator of the Stedelijk Museum,
for his invaluable advice and devoted collaboration.

PRINTED IN JAPAN BY ZOKEISHA PUBLICATIONS LTD., TOKYO

What is man that thou art mindful of him?

and the son of man that thou visitest him?

CHARLOTTE SALOMON'S PAINTINGS were shown me on one of the most agitated days in my life — a day of festive celebration. Suddenly all movement around me ceased, giving way to an inner movement: I was drawn into a human life that began and ended far away, but in which nothing was strange to me. For in these pictures and notes there is something universally human, something that bridges the distance between man and man. But what makes this life a true symbol is something more than its universality. It is specifically the life of a very gifted and sensitive young woman, lived in one of the most terrible periods of European history, that speaks in the almost primitive simplicity of these pictures. One reason why they are so expressive is that instead of concentrating on the horrors of the end, they tell a life story that is close to our own experience. Against the background of this story, Charlotte's fate—known to us from others—moves us all the more deeply. Books such as this will long be a needed reminder to a mankind that relapses so easily into the indifference and triviality of daily life. They remind us of what we are always tempted to forget, namely, that the value of a human life does not consist in its length, but in its substance and message. And the short life of Charlotte Salomon has a great deal to tell us through this book.

PAUL TILLICH

EDITORIAL NOTE

CHARLOTTE WAS BORN in Berlin on April 16, 1917, the only child of Dr. Albert Salomon and his wife Franziska. At the age of nine she lost her mother. Four years later her father married Paula Lindberg, a well-known singer.

. In 1933, when Charlotte was sixteen, her sheltered life came to a sudden end. She refused to stay in school where as a Jewess she was subjected to all sorts of humiliations. But in 1935 she was admitted to the State Academy of Fine Arts. In the course of her studies, she was awarded the Academy Prize, though for "racial reasons" the award was later revoked. In 1939 her father decided to send her to her maternal grandparents, who had already emigrated and were living in Villefranche in southern France. Here, he thought, she would be safe.

Beginning in 1940, in the greatest loneliness and distress, Charlotte tried to re-capture a sense of reality and continuity by telling the story of her life and that of her family in pictures. Of this record, almost a thousand gouaches were preserved, beginning with the betrothal of her parents and ending with her life as a refugee in southern France. Years later, Charlotte's father, who with his wife had survived the war in Holland, came into possession of the pictures, which he donated to the Stedelijk Museum in Amsterdam.

This book shows a selection of eighty of the pictures, giving the essence of her life. The texts are Charlotte's; she had pasted them on the pictures or written them on directly. The Bible quotation prefacing the book recurs a number of times in Charlotte's notes. Dr. Emil Straus, a German refugee in Nice who knew Charlotte Salomon and her grandparents, the Grünwalds, well during their stay in Nice-Villefranche, has kindly contributed the following account of Charlotte's life while she was working on these pictures and afterward, up to the moment of her deportation.

BIOGRAPHICAL NOTE

I · THE HERMITAGE

THE LAST YEARS of Charlotte Salomon's life would have been very different but for her grandparents' trip to Spain. For it was there that Dr. Grünwald and his wife Marianne made friends with Mrs. Moore, an American of German extraction. A widow in her early middle years, Mrs. Moore lived in a beautiful villa in Villefranche near Nice, surrounded by a garden full of flowers of all kinds, pepper trees, cypresses, olive and orange trees—an oasis of peace. A far cry from the turmoil and horror of National Socialist Berlin, which Mrs. Moore visited all unsuspecting in February, 1933, drawn chiefly by her interest in the theater.

In Berlin she went to see her friends the Grünwalds. It was from their living-room window that on March 1, 1933, she witnessed the historical torchlight parade in honor of the National Socialist seizure of power.

The elderly physician and his wife were frightened and depressed. They told their American friend what it meant to be Jewish in Hitler Germany. With typical American generosity, Mrs. Moore invited the Grünwalds to visit her at the Hermitage, as her villa in Villefranche was called, and stay as long as they pleased. There was a three-room cottage shaded by pines at the far end of the garden, and they could have it all to themselves.

At first the Grünwalds, with their Prussian sense of what was fitting and proper, had no thought of accepting. But that same year they left Germany, where, as the Nazis became firmly entrenched, the persecution of the Jews increased. First they went to Rome. Intelligent and well read, interested in history and archaeology, Mrs. Grünwald tried, in her new surroundings, to forget the terrors of the recent past. But the couple's finances were limited, and it soon became evident that the National Socialist regime was not going to blow over in a few months, as they had originally hoped.

The two old people decided to accept Mrs. Moore's offer, and in the spring of 1934 they moved into her cottage in Villefranche. Eager to study Italian and French, Dr. Grünwald discovered the Nice Centre Universitaire, a branch of the University of Aix-en-Provence. I was teaching there at the time, and one day he turned up in my class.

We became acquainted and I soon discovered that his son-in-law, Dr. Salomon, was married to the singer Paula Lindberg, who had been my fellow musician at one time. A friendship grew up between us. We exchanged visits which were extremely enjoyable, owing largely to Mrs. Grünwald, with her keen mind and artistic and scholarly interests. And so they passed five years (1934-1939) in the paradise of the Hermitage. Thanks to a faithful housekeeper, Mrs. Grünwald had ample time in which to read and to enjoy the Mediterranean countryside. "How that woman spoiled my grandmother," Charlotte told me later. "I shall always be grateful to her for it."

IN THE SPRING of 1939 the Grünwalds' granddaughter, Charlotte Salomon, a girl of twenty-two, arrived at their haven. Her father, also a physician, had recently been released from the Sachsenhausen concentration camp, broken in health; he and his wife were preparing to leave the country. Their plans for the future were uncertain. It was decided that Charlotte should join her grandparents.

One day her grandmother brought her to see me, and there she stood, slender, blue-eyed, with tousled ash-blonde hair and red cheeks, all youth and freshness, a trifle awkward in her movements, and as timid as a fawn. She scrutinized me distrustfully, but showed a certain interest when she learned that I had known her stepmother, Paula, as a young girl. Her father's second wife was a big problem in her life—one she had never solved. She was more outgoing toward my wife than to me. But she was obviously eager to leave. The conversation was of no interest to her. The only thing that absorbed her for the moment was the southern landscape. All this light and color were new to her and struck a profound chord in her mystical, sensitive nature.

She was delighted to be living at the Hermitage. All day long she sat in the garden, drawing and painting. Or she would lie for hours under an orange tree, looking into the blue sky. Sometimes she fell asleep, and awoke drunk with happiness.

She took little part in the life of the household. She lived in her world of light, air, and color; she did drawings with pencil and charcoal, India ink, or crayon, and now and then a delicate, fragrant water color: scenes in the garden, on the beach, on the street. Wherever she happened to be, she pulled out her sketchbook. She had to unburden herself, and her language was pencil or brush. "Art," she wrote on one of her drawings, "is an act of self-abandonment, my only hope of escaping the loneliness that is the lot of all human beings."

In company she was unsure of herself. She detested having to talk, and especially answering questions about herself. Her grandparents thought her stupid and sullen but that was not the case; she was a sensitive young woman with a deep artistic feeling and an intense emotional life. The hardships and danger of her life in Berlin were forgotten. She had recovered her calm and inner balance. Her thoughts and feelings found the medium they needed in the freedom of her new surroundings. As her inner assurance grew, she derived increasing satisfaction from her art work. She was still shy and closed in, but gradually Mrs. Moore won her confidence, and she began to speak to her of her life and work. Every morning while Mrs. Moore had her breakfast, Charlotte settled on the rug by her bedside.

Years before, Mrs. Moore had taken ten Jewish children, some of them orphans, into her house, where they were fed, clothed, and cared for. They attended public school in Villefranche and received private instruction in music, drawing, and gymnastics. Charlotte herself wrote: "What depth of compassion, to take poor homeless creatures like us into her house and care for us as her own!"

Mrs. Moore bought a number of Charlotte's pictures, to sell in America—or so she said. This gave Charlotte pocket money and increased her self-confidence.

Little by little, Charlotte gained confidence in me. The interest I showed in her drawing and painting won her over. She came to feel that my sympathy was sincere and that I really tried to understand her. She often came to see us in Nice; we spoke for hours about painting, poetry, and music (an art that she loved as much as her own), about her work at the Berlin Academy, and of course about the war and political events. We even spoke about the meaning of life, a subject with which she like so many young girls of her generation was deeply concerned. I discovered not only a profound lover of painting and music, but also an uncommonly intelligent and independent-minded young girl. Once she brought me one of her light, airy pastels— a little boy fishing. She tried to say it was a present, stammered a few words, and turned as red as a lobster. I understood her and was touched by her confidence in me. After that her inhibitions were gone, she opened up completely. She came to see me when she was unhappy and treated me almost like a second father.

In September, 1939, the war broke out. All France was on the brink of despair. Threatening cries of "Our Nice," "Mare Nostrum," came across from nearby Italy. Many French families left the coast in haste.

Charlotte was deeply shaken. Surrounded by hopelessness, she felt once again that the bottom had fallen out of her world. She did not get along too well with her grandparents, and sometimes there were open quarrels. This was no mere conflict between generations, but something more deep-seated. They were profoundly different in temperament and had been molded by radically different worlds. Charlotte grew sad and lonelier than ever. She looked within. "I know my feelings are right, because they were born of such unspeakably dark hours."

On another occasion she wrote: "It is my nature as a human being to remind people of the suffering they would so gladly turn away from. But I have never forgotten to make it plain that I love life with all my heart. And to love life, you have to consider its dark side—death—you must include suffering in your thoughts and understand it. To all those whom I love I wish hard experiences that will make them look within themselves. For to feel compassion for others, we must have borne our own cross. It is indispensable for any human or artistic achievement in life. But just take a look at the people of today . . ." And on another page: "People were no longer able to listen to each other, but began at once to speak of themselves. And so a being who suffered, but was able to rise a little above her suffering, conceived a feeling that people are utterly helpless, grasping at straws amid the most fearful deluge."

Yet she loved life passionately. She was young and strong, capable of putting up a fight when necessary. She saw the misery, horror, shame, and fear of all those around her. People were so worried about their own skins that they became morbidly indifferent to others. There was no end in sight. Without resources or civil rights, the refugees felt utterly homeless. Unable to bear her sufferings any longer, old Mrs. Grünwald took her own life—a cruel, heart-rending moment for all those who had been close to this noble, intelligent, sensitive woman. She had expressed the wish that I speak at her grave. It was a sorrowful little procession that followed her to the cemetery in Nice.

Charlotte stood rigid and lifeless by the open grave. Grandfather Grünwald bore his immense sorrow with courage and restraint. Now he was alone with Charlotte, but the difference in their characters stood between them. An imposing figure, with his well-kept white beard à la Bernard Shaw, Dr. Grünwald was an aristocrat in nature and appearance. His bearing, his calm, considered speech, his conciliatory attitude toward others, gave the impression of great self-assurance. The collapse of his world and all its values after eighty years of security, prosperity, and respected social position had made him indifferent to the present. He lived in an imaginary world, took little interest in the life around him, and sought refuge more and more in a past where Charlotte could not follow him. Their life together became unbearable. Dr. Grünwald moved into Nice, Charlotte stayed on in Villefranche.

May, 1940. The German offensive had overrun France. Thousands of refugees, both French and foreign, came swarming to the coast; Jews from many European countries, who had been living in Holland, Belgium, and particularly in Paris, sought safety in southern France. Italy's entrance into the war in June, 1940, increased the confusion in our region that was so close to the border. An Italian offensive was expected and the French authorities lost their heads in the fear of a fifth column. All foreigners were compelled to leave the *département*. Like thousands of other fugitives, Grandfather Grünwald and Charlotte were sent to Gurs in the Pyrenees, where a camp had been improvised. Living conditions were unspeakable, the food was insufficient and inedible, and the sleeping quarters ghastly in every respect. Fortunately, the oldest inmates were discharged in July. And on July 12th, Charlotte was permitted to leave with her grandfather. Overjoyed, they returned to the Hermitage. "God, how beautiful it is here," she cried out. It was then that she began to work on her pictorial diary. In the course of the next two years she did a thousand gouaches and any number of pastels and water colors. She was so possessed with her art that she scarcely ate, drank, or slept. She decided to tell the story of her past in pictures. On one of the last sheets she noted: "It was then that I began to work on these leaves. I was very unhappy. Certain people filled me with a nearly paralyzing despair. . . . People in general became intolerable to me. My only recourse was to cut myself off more than ever in the hope of finding what I had to find, myself. . . . The war was still raging, and there I sat by the sea, looking deep into the hearts of those who made up my world. I was my mother, my grandmother; in fact, I myself was all the people who appear in my work. I learned to live their lives and so became myself. The months passed and it seemed that my work would never be done. My grandfather wrote to me often. . . ."

Her creative passion gave her no rest. Her search for herself forged the divergent elements of her work into a remarkable unity. The apocalyptic disintegrating world, the sweet serenity of nature, her profound identification with the characters of her story, and finally her growing self-awareness—all these became one in her experience. It was this experience that she expressed in terms of line and color.

III · THE DIARY

IT HAS BEEN NECESSARY to limit the present book to a selection from the many gouaches. To what extent the chronological sequence follows that of the events depicted is hard to determine. In the process of finding herself, Charlotte looked back over her childhood. Through the death of her mother, she had been turned over to governesses or her grandparents. Loneliness had made her aloof, unable to confide in others; hypersensitive, in love with nature and art, she had lived in a private dream world.

And now, in her oasis surrounded by a world of confusion and despair, Charlotte became clearly conscious of things which up until then she had felt only intuitively. She opened her heart and poured forth the images she had been storing up for so long—at a headlong pace, never stopping to rest, as though suspecting how little time she had ahead of her.

Charlotte's pictures all center around the human figure or, it might be more accurate to say, the human being himself, whom she sees with a wonderful immediacy. And in the self-portraits she discloses the same unclouded vision of herself. A whole life unrolls before us—childhood, early love, political and family events, and finally her years at the Hermitage with all their joy and horror.

IV · THE END

ON SEPTEMBER 27, 1941, Mrs. Moore left Villefranche for America with ten of her adoptive children, her daughter, and a nephew. Life became increasingly difficult. Food was severely rationed. The only hope of getting halfway enough to eat was through the black market, and that was very expensive.

"Mrs. Moore left me a friend," Charlotte wrote at the time; "I didn't quite know what to do with him." This was Alexander Nagler, who had moved into the Hermitage to take care of the four remaining children, two of them French and two Belgians. The French children were not Jews; the two little Belgians were later taken away by their parents. Old Dr. Grünwald stayed on in Nice but frequently moved back to the Hermitage for weeks on end, especially in the wintertime.

It would happen that Charlotte and her grandfather did not exchange a word for days. In her grandfather's eyes she was a sulky dreamer who cared only for her art and took no interest in his existence. Charlotte, for her part, thought her grandfather a stuffy old egotist, concerned only with his personal comfort. I tried my best to reconcile them and sometimes was successful. But no sooner had I left them than the bickering resumed. Everyone's nerves were on edge. It became more and more difficult to procure a minimum of food for the household. The black market swallowed up the last of people's resources, and the end of the war did not seem in sight. In the fall of 1942, after the American landing in Morocco, the whole French coast as far as Marseilles was occupied by Italian troops and the OVRA (the Italian Secret Police). The Jewish refugees and many of the French lived in terror. It became dangerous to go out in the street because of the patrols that stopped people at random and asked for their papers. The Italians began deporting people. The OVRA worked hand in glove with the Gestapo and took to offering rewards for the denunciation of foreign refugees. The police took a census of the Jews and stamped the word "Jew" on their identity papers. Spies and informers were everywhere. By the end of the war, eight thousand persons had been arrested in Nice alone, some sent to labor camps and others to concentration camps in Germany. Very few of them ever returned.

All this fear and hardship was too much for Grandfather Grünwald. He became so weak that he could barely stand. One day he collapsed in the street. Friendly neighbors took him to his lodgings in Nice, and there he quietly died. On February 12, 1943, we buried him.

Alexander Nagler now had only the French children to take care of. This imposing, well-built Austrian had formerly been a businessman. He took a keen interest in Charlotte's work. In these chaotic, uncertain times, he gave her a certain sense of security. They were living alone in the big house, and he was almost the only human being with whom Charlotte could speak. There were occasional visits among neighbors, especially Dr. M., a physician with whom they had made friends, but as the danger increased, such visits became more and more infrequent. Nagler and Charlotte became dependent on each other; he was her companion, protector, and friend. Probably he was the first man in her life. She had made up her mind to become his wife, but while her grandfather was alive she had been unable to gain his consent: Professor Grünwald considered Nagler beneath the Grünwalds in social station. But Alexander Nagler and Charlotte loved each other. Now the old man was dead, and in May, 1943, they were married at the Town Hall in Nice. Dr. M. and his wife were the witnesses. Nagler had procured a suckling kid for the wedding breakfast at the Hermitage. Vittoria Bravi, the faithful housekeeper, had set a magnificent table with company china and silverware. All were in high spirits. Charlotte looked fresh and happy.

But Nagler had made a serious blunder. Dr. M., who had been his friend for years and had often helped him in times of need, had provided him with a new identity card without the stamp "Jew." When Nagler applied to the police for a marriage license, the official in charge informed him that he as an Aryan could not marry a Jewish girl. Beside himself with rage, Nagler blurted out that he too was Jewish. He received permission to marry, but was obliged to leave his faked identity card with his exact address at Police Headquarters. This was his undoing. When he told the doctor what had happened, his friend was horrified and advised Nagler and his young wife to leave the Hermitage at once and to move to a vacant apartment he had in Nice, which he offered them free of charge. Charlotte and Nagler stayed there for a while, but the Hermitage, with all its beauties, especially in the summer, drew them irresistibly back to Villefranche.

On September 8, 1943, after Italy had concluded a separate armistice with the Allies, German troops occupied the coast. The Police Headquarters and Town Hall were at once placed under control of the Gestapo.

At seven o'clock in the evening of September 21, 1943, a Gestapo truck drew up outside the Hermitage. Charlotte and her husband were dragged out of the house and thrown into the truck. . . . Loud cries were heard . . . and that was all. It was the end. They both died in the gas chambers of Auschwitz.

EMIL STRAUS

CHARLOTTE: A DIARY IN PICTURES

Charlotte's mother, Franziska, who was a volunteer nurse in the First World War, presents her fiancé, a surgeon whom she met in a military hospital, to her parents.

In the presence of the witnesses, the registrar of the German Empire places the ring on the finger of the long, slender hand of the happy bride.

After the civil marriage, dressmaker and assistant hover around Franziska and arrange her wedding gown. She is radiant as she walks on the arm of her beloved, followed by the numerous wedding party.

Barely a year later, the war was at an end. Franziska's husband Albert returned unexpectedly, shortly before the birth of their first child. She gave it the name Charlotte, in memory of her deceased sister, and mailed the announcement to all their friends and relatives.

Though little Charlotte did not seem overjoyed at being born, for she yelled pitifully day and night, Franziska was delighted. She nursed her herself and was disappointed each time the domineering nurse took the baby from her. She also insisted on pushing the tall white baby carriage, watching carefully over the tiny head of the new Charlotte.

Then came the day when Franziska took Charlotte to school. Charlotte didn't particularly like it. The teacher started to scold her the moment she looked around. But she made a friend there, Kurt, with black curly hair.

Her birthday was always a great occasion. The whole class was invited, for coffee and supper. Kurt made a big speech and ended by asking the guests to drink to Charlotte's health.

But Christmas was even nicer. Charlotte's mother sat at the piano and sang "Silent Night, Holy Night," and her father and grandparents sang along with her, and so did Charlotte and the maids, who stood next to the tree which Franziska had trimmed. While the singing went on, Charlotte kept peeping stealthily at the big laundry basket that stood in the middle of the room. It contained, as always, the most unexpectedly wonderful presents.

Charlotte greatly enjoyed winter sports; she was especially good at ice skating.

The apartment was truly beautiful. It consisted of:

Her father's study with adjoining consulting room.

The drawing room, all in blue, with her mother's piano.

The big dining room, with an alcove in the background which was used for the less important meals such as breakfast and afternoon coffee.

A long hallway led to the rear part of the apartment.

There was the storage room with all the well-stocked linen closets.

The nursery for the expected offspring.

The bedroom.

The kitchen in which Augusta, the cook, sat and waited for orders from the lady of the house.

The bathroom.

On her first trip, Charlotte was taken to the Bavarian mountains. She thought of it often in later years. Her mother was very gay and ran around with her a lot. Her father was rather serious, but he joined them in boating and mountain climbing.

Charlotte's mother was highly emotional. Often she took the child to bed with her and told her stories about life after death in heaven. This sounded wonderful, and Franziska seemed to long for it nostalgically. Repeatedly she asked Charlotte if it would not be nice to have her mother be an angel with wings. Charlotte agreed with her that that would indeed be nice. But she asked her mother not to forget her once she was in heaven and to come down as an angel to bring her a letter and place it on the window sill. She was to write her exactly what it was like up there in heaven.

Then, all of a sudden, Charlotte's mother ceased to take pleasure in anything. All she talked of was dying. Her husband pleaded with her: he needed her, and so did little Charlotte, who was still so young. Only eight years old. But it didn't help.

"My husband doesn't love me, my child doesn't need me. What, then, am I living for?" These were her thoughts.

Franziska was unwilling to go on living. One night she got up, went to her husband's medicine chest, and took out a strong dose of opium which she swallowed. Then she went back to bed.

"What on earth are you trying do? What an idea, to poison yourself! Thank God it didn't come off." The dose hadn't been strong enough and her husband's efforts brought her back to life.

Since it was felt that she might be more peaceful in her parents' house than in her own, her husband and her father took her there.

A neurologist was consulted who found her perfectly normal and attributed her attempted suicide to a passing phase of hysteria.

For a long time she stood at the window, dreamy and full of longing.

Now she stands there no longer, she has gone to another place.

Alas, I have lost her, alas, we have lost her . . .

Many people came to the funeral. But Albert felt forsaken and alone as he stood by her coffin, which was to be cremated.

The grandparents and Charlotte did not go to the funeral. Charlotte asked her grandmother why everybody was crying. If her mother was now an angel in heaven, one should rejoice in her happiness and not weep for her. This remark made a strange impression on the grandmother.

When, a few weeks after the funeral, they visited the grave, the little girl took along a letter for her mother. She asked her not to forget her promise and to let her know as quickly and thoroughly as possible "what it was like up there in heaven." For the first time her father almost smiled.

Charlotte could not sleep properly any more. She got up ten times at night to see whether there was any trace of an angelic visit, or at least a letter on the window sill.

A governess appeared. "Do this, do that." Charlotte did her best to annoy her and thought up all kinds of mischief. When she got slapped, she immediately announced it to her grandmother over the telephone. And when her grandmother came she would be told, to Charlotte's delight, that nobody could put up with such a dreadful child.

"I don't need any governess, I know best what I want."

But to her dismay, a new governess appeared, far worse than the first one. Charlotte was desperate. At school, also, she was often slapped. It distressed her father, but there was nothing he could do about it.

Finally, Charlotte had her way. A young girl, Hase by name, took the place of the elderly governesses. Charlotte was delighted with her new companion. Hase played the mandolin and she decided that Charlotte had a gift for drawing. Christmas was as marvelous as ever, with many presents and a Christmas tree.

Charlotte was very proud of her father. He liked good food and he thought it might be a good idea to marry again. Because of the many possibilities the choice was hard. At a party he met a singer who sang a song by Schubert. Her singing made a strong impression on him. They talked together, and he told her that he had a little girl. This pleased her very much.

The singer had the delightful name Paulinka. She came to see them almost every night, and Charlotte and her father looked forward eagerly to her visits. Charlotte could not think of anything but Paulinka Bimbam, but she was too embarrassed to let anyone else know it.

Albert and Paulinka decided to marry. While they were on their wedding trip, Charlotte stayed with her grandparents. When she was taken back to her home, Charlotte could not bring herself to ring the doorbell and struggled with her escort until she was so annoyed that she went up the stairs to ring the bell herself. Ashamed at last, Charlotte rushed up the stairs where her dearly beloved Paulinka stood in a black dress and embraced her tenderly.

At a reception in her home, Paulinka sings the Bach aria:

"Strike, o strike, awaited hour!"

"Everyone loves her—but nobody as much as I do."

On the next two pages:

Paulinka's mother has died: in silence and mourning, the family sits around the table.

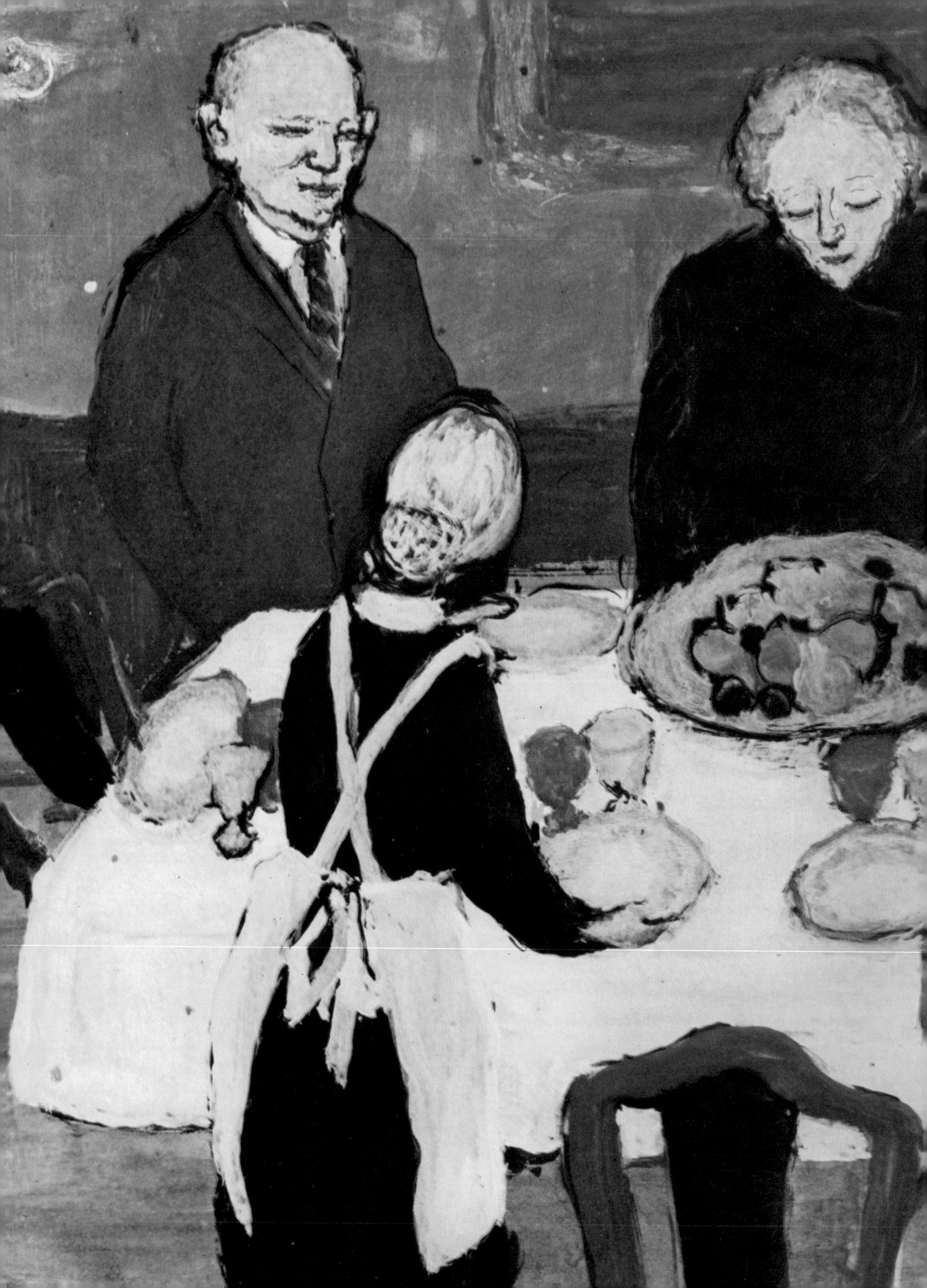

Paulinka could not rid herself of the feeling that little Charlotte might someday also throw herself out of the window. It seemed quite clear to her that the strict upbringing of the grandmother had stifled some natural impulses in her children and created tensions in them which only death could resolve. After the usual tender good night to her husband she declared: "Grandmother won't get this child. I shall protect her myself."

Charlotte and Paulinka have their first disagreement—and their first reconciliation.

January 30, 1933

"Millions look to the swastika with hope,
The day of liberty and bread is dawning."

The swastika makes its appearance in the school also. Charlotte tells her father: "I won't go to school any more, no matter what you say or do."

Charlotte gets her way and has private drawing lessons.

Charlotte's grandparents travel a great deal and they invite their granddaughter to join them in Italy.

"And then we sat in a small inn in the Roman Campagna and had lunch
there and drank red wine and I was happy and the wisteria was in
bloom, it was spring, and yesterday—I had my seventeenth birthday."

After many difficulties the State Academy of Fine Arts accepted Charlotte as a pupil although she was Jewish. Her joy bursts forth in radiant colors.

Working frantically, she made good progress in her studies and her teachers were pleased with her.

She even made friends with Barbara.

This is Barbara, much beloved by everybody.

A new person entered into Charlotte's life—Daberlohn, a voice teacher. He accompanied Paulinka and discussed his theories with her.

Coming home from the Academy, Charlotte sees Daberlohn's hat and coat in the hall.

Daberlohn and the adored Paulinka are absorbed in their music —
Charlotte is superfluous.

No one pays attention to her.

Daberlohn accompanies Paulinka on her way to rehearsal—
Charlotte is left behind.

On the next two pages:
Charlotte is busy with a book which she plans to illustrate as a
birthday gift for Daberlohn, who fascinates her.

Daberlohn: "The illustrations must be finished in time for my birthday, September 23rd. So you have six months. Why do you look at me like that? Don't you want to give me a birthday present?"

ZU MEINEM
GEBURTS-
TAG
AM

23.

SIE
HABEN
ALSO
NOCH

EIN
HALBE
JAHR
ZE

MBER

MÜSSEN

DIE

WAS
MACHEN
SIE DENN
FÜR EIN
KOMISCHE
GESIC

ONEN

FRTIG
SEIN

WOLLE
SIE
MIR
ZU MEINE
GEBURTSTA
NICHS
SCHE
KEN?

Charlotte worked day and night on the illustrations. "Softly the hour trickles into the dream of night."

Charlotte tries to express in an etching what attracts her unconsciously so strongly to Daberlohn. With concentrated intensity she works on the illustrations.

"Even if I go crazy, I have to get it the way I want. The proof isn't right yet."

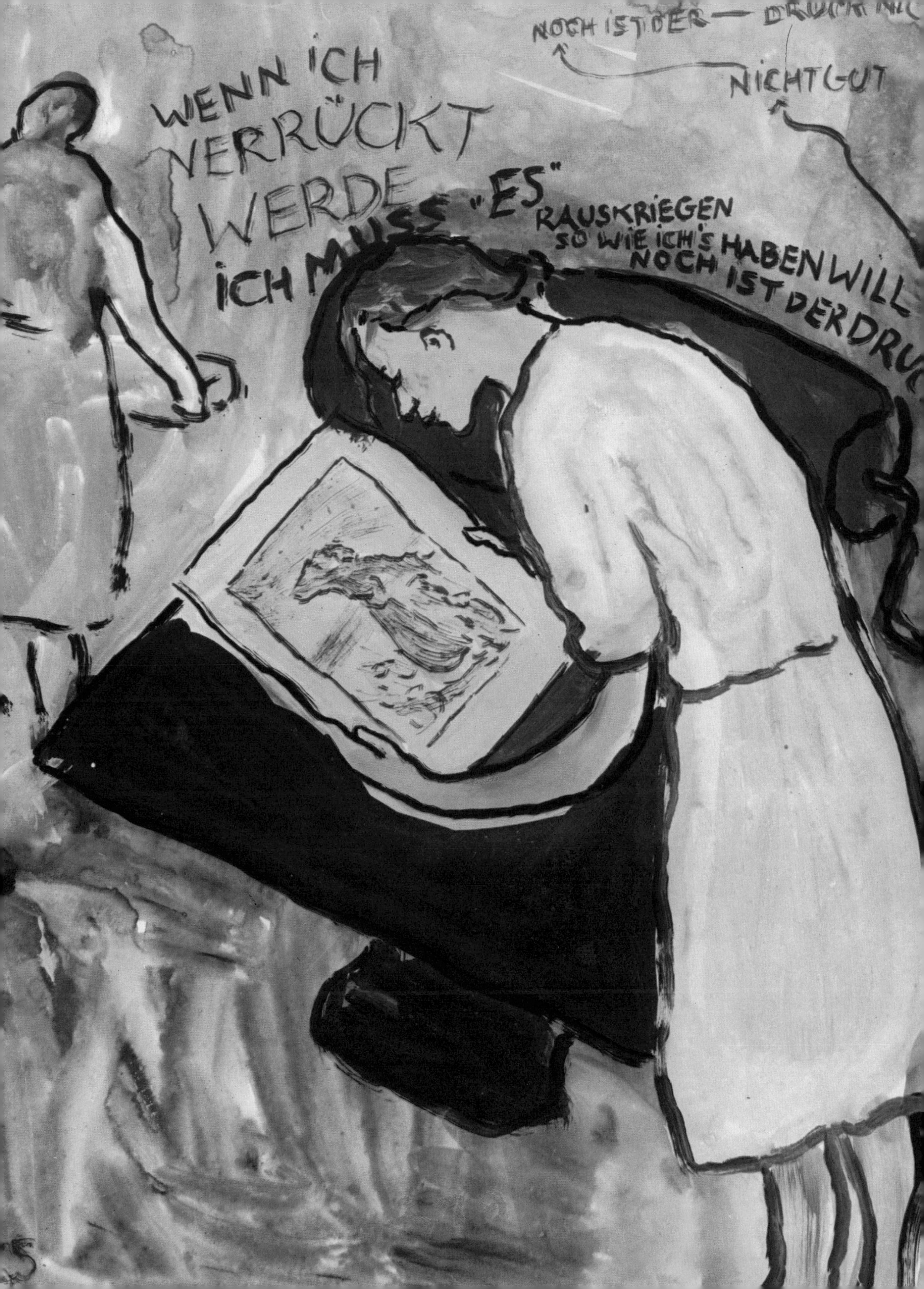

"At least I'll know whether he likes my drawings."

Charlotte showed Daberlohn her drawings:

"Which one would you like?"

After a brief but concentrated study he picked out the meadow with the yellow buttercups. He also selected another drawing and asked her to give him both.

"I would."

JCH MÖCHTE GERNE AUCH "DEN TOD UND DAS MÄDCHEN" HABEN
DAS SIND "WIR BEIDE"

"I am giving you only this one."

Daberlohn to Charlotte: "To love life completely one must also accept and understand its other side, death and sorrow. I wish everyone I love the experience of suffering so that they are forced to find the way to their depths."

"I picked it for him—it is said to bring luck."

"Out with the Jews!"

"I just confiscated a first-rate fountain pen at Cohn's."

"Vengeance on the Jews and destruction to their temples."

"Great is Jehovah, trust in him."

"Really, one is ashamed to be a German."

"Now we can breathe again, the air is clear of Jews."

"Germans, beware, you will have to atone for this."

Some time later, Charlotte's father was taken away to a concentration camp.

Charlotte went to the police station to make inquiries about her father.
The square was filled with anxious women.

"We want to know where our men are."

"How should we know where your men are,
Go home, or we'll catch you too,
Go home, you little pig of a Jew."

WIR WOLLEN WISSEN
WO
UNSERE MÄNNER
SIND

WIE ---
SOLL'N WIR ---
WISSEN
WO
EURE MÄNNER SIND
GEH NACH HAUSE
SONST SPERRT MAN
DICH NOCH EIN
GEH NACH HAUSE
DU KLEINES JUDENSCH...

EINTRITT
VERBOT...

The former professor and surgeon is made to do heavy manual labor. "You've got to work here, no loafing around."

"You've taken it easy long enough."

GE-
FAU-
LENZT
HABT
IHR
GENUG
IN
EUREM
LEBEN

As a singer, Paulinka had much influence and many friends; she eventually succeeded in obtaining the release of her husband, who came home again.

The grandparents had emigrated from Germany some time ago and found refuge in the south of France. Now they invited Charlotte to join them.

The Grandmother: "What has to be done must be done. I will write her at once that we shall do everything to have Charlotte with us as soon as possible."

Charlotte's Father: "I will send her away."

The Grandparents: "How wonderful, he is sending her to us, how very glad we are."

Charlotte is once again under the spell of Daberlohn's charm. She worries and wonders whether she will have the chance to say good-by to him.

In a dream, she imagines their farewell.

The Father: "And here is my picture to remember me by."

UND ZUM ABSCHIED
SCHENKE ICH DIR HIER
MEIN BILD

The last evening in her own room.

"All aboard."

Life with the grandparents is not an easy one.

The Grandfather: "Can't you do anything but draw? Your grandmother is much too good to you. Why shouldn't you take a job as a maid like all the others?"

The Grandmother: "But just look at her—isn't she melancholy personified as it is?"

Charlotte was put to do housework.

"I hate them all—how I wish I could be rid of them!"

September 1939.

"The German troops have crossed the Rhineland border. War is declared. It appears that England will follow suit."

One evening the seventy-year-old grandmother gave vent to her despair:

"Pain and terror overshadow the world,

The rule of law and reason is suspended,

Friendship and trust are destroyed.

There is no meaning left to life,

No sense in asking why and wherefor.

But just as Nature dies and is reborn,

So will our ashes come to life again."

The grandmother now withdrew completely into herself.

She did not weep but seemed lost in an abyss. Sorrow was diffused from the tip of her hair down to the toes of her small feet. She passed beyond her personal suffering and assumed the suffering of the whole world. The burden was too much to bear.

She tried to kill herself, but was found in time.

"Thank God, she is not yet dead."

Though Charlotte watched over her and talked to her about the beauty around them—the sea, the sky, the sun—the grandmother slipped away in an unwatched moment and threw herself out of the window, like her daughter.

"I cannot bear this life, I cannot bear these times."

NOTICE

All German nationals have to leave the city and *département* without delay.

"You know, Grandfather, I feel as though the world is in pieces and needs to be put together again."

On the road.

Charlotte: "God, how beautiful it is here!"

The Grandfather: "Oh, do come on, after all we have to find a place to sleep tonight."

"God, my God, how beautiful it is."

And she saw, as if awakening from a dream, all the beauty around her, saw the sea, felt the sun, and knew: She must disappear from the world of men for a while and sacrifice all in order to re-create a new world for herself, from the depths.

Date Due

Jan			
Jan			

Demco 293-5